Motivate

Charts and Pictures that Help Children with A.D.H.D. Focus and Organize

By Katie Unterreiner, MSW, LCSW

Contents

Introduction

Most children between the ages of 5 and 12 are challenged by demands to focus and organize, and even more so for children with A.D.H.D. or other learning differences. This book is a toolkit of fun learning strategies to help inspire and motivate these children who struggle through their daily transitions at home and school.

In this book, I use a blend of positive words, visuals and charts to highlight the stories, words and movements that keep families strong, focused and connected during times of transition. I started using pictures and charts as an in-home social worker for families referred to me by Child Protective Services. I used pictures to help families plan and create an environment that supported kindness and healing. Many of the children that I worked with struggled with social skills, planning and organization. I helped children develop important executive function skills which nurture learning and growth at home and school. Executive function skills help children stop actions, notice and plan their own behavior and adapt to changing situations. These pictures, charts and supportive words help children develop executive function which enables families to connect and organize home life. I later tailored this curriculum for my own son and children like him who struggled with inattention and sensory related issues. The charts and routines included in this book helped my son become motivated to learn new and important social and organization skills. Following is a short description of the learning strategies used in this book.

Charts for Daily Routines

There are four charts representing typical daily routine: morning, homework, dinner and bedtime. These charts help families organize and stay on task during a busy school year. Each routine is made up of five steps. Each step is represented with a picture and days of the week to help track your child's effort. Each routine has a unique set of three pictures that act as a measure for your child's effort. I use the words 'needs work,' 'good' and 'great' to go along with the pictures on the top of the pages of morning, homework, dinner and bedtime routine. Although the pictures are different for each routine they all have the same language about effort and hard work to acknowledge the intention and focus that goes into the steps that are a part of each routine.

Supportive Statements and Questions

There are certain types of conversation and praise that support these daily routines. Using family storytelling strategies and praise focused on effort are a part of each one of these charts. Supportive words create a positive narrative for the way we think and interpret the many parts of routine such as brushing teeth or preparing for sleep. Children who listen to family stories and hear process-based praise are more capable of influencing and creating positive change in their own lives. Process-based praise is supportive language related to effort or process, rather than outcome, that helps children understand their ability to thrive and be creative. Also included with each routine are questions for families to pose to one another, ideas for conversation and statements that support children's hard work and focus during different parts of the day. These statements and words are infused with empathy, kindness and motivation for your child and family.

House Meeting Charts

The house meeting charts use visuals and words to help families connect and review progress with daily routines. The house meeting is also a time to talk about how your family can support one another and what strategies can be used to help everyone do their best. The house meeting is one of the most powerful charts as it allows family to review their progress and express thanks and appreciation for one another. There is a sheet of strengths that reflect the values and emotional skills being developed. Each person can pick a strength that

will help them grow in the coming week. These strengths develop positive character and self-esteem.

The house meeting helps family members look at how routines can be improved upon or maintained through the coming week. The final part of the house meeting is choosing a weekly or daily chore. It's helpful to talk about how chores and routines went during the week and praise family members for working together to take care of the home. The pictures and words on this chart make choosing a chore simple and fun.

Emotional Skills

Strong emotions and difficulty connecting and bonding can interfere with daily routines and create general discord among family members. There are several visuals to help families talk and work through strong emotions and develop strategies to resolve conflict. A weather wheel and associated questions help children identify and understand their feelings. A series of sparkle activities are included to help your child respond more positively in difficult situations. Finally, techniques for managing stress and its impact on your child's body are addressed with feeling signals and relaxation exercises.

Pictures as Tools for Organization

Picture charts and positive words communicate beautifully and completely the story of each transition and behavior that make up morning, homework, dinner and bedtime routines. The pictures in this book breathe fun and soul into the work that goes into preparing for school or connecting as a family. As a social worker, I use pictures and charts to nurture communication among family members and clarify goals. Children relate better to words and feelings when they are connected to pictures and deeper stories.

Morning Routine

It's easy to see the cloud of poor motivation and frustration that looms over children as they struggle to wake up and prepare for a difficult day of learning. Morning time involves some inspiration and motivation. The pictures in this chart provide clear cues for each expected behavior that make up the morning routine.

The struggle children anticipate facing at school, particularly those with learning differences, is often expressed in stress and resistance to each part of getting ready. This stress can set in motion a negative and unstructured routine. Picture charts and positive words inspire a more organized and focused transition to school. It's helpful to wake up at least an hour before leaving to school to give you and your child time to step through morning routine. Here is some information about each step that helps create an organized and peaceful morning time routine.

Wake Up

The pictures in this chart serve as a cue for each part of morning routine. Pictures themselves help children focus and feel a sense of calm. This chart allows each child to take ownership of the morning routine leaving less space for arguing and friction between parent and child. I recommend putting the morning chart up in your child's room before wake up to serve as a prompt. It's nice to wake up to a pleasant scent. Aromatherapy is a helpful way to focus the energy and creativity of children. It's helpful to vary the scent to keep children's interest.

Getting Dressed

Getting dressed is represented with a picture of pants and a shirt. This visual serves as a cue for your child to pick out his or her clothes and get dressed. It's important to look at the morning chart together to help focus on the steps ahead. It's helpful to put a pleasant essential oil on your child's shirt to help engage the senses in a pleasing way. This is also a good time to take several cleansing breaths. Breathing in for three seconds and then breathing out for three seconds helps your child feel relaxed and helps them regulate their body against stress. Putting a small stuffed animal on your child's tummy helps your child regulate breathing and see more clearly their tummy rise and fall with each breath. It's also helpful to have your child meditate on the importance of choosing positive and hopeful words to start the day. These positive words will help direct his or her energy and help push out negative thoughts and behavior.

Breakfast

Children with inattention may have difficulty transitioning to breakfast. I recommend putting a positive note or looking at the strength sheet together. Words and pictures identifying your child's strengths can spark fun conversations. Identifying strengths supports positive character development and nurtures kindness. There is a list of strengths included in the section on house meetings. You may also want to put a funny animal picture next to his or her place to add some novelty to the morning time routine.

Getting Ready for School

Organizing to leave for school is the last picture of this routine. I have a picture of shoes, lunch box and a backpack for this final step of morning routine. It's helpful to stand together by the door and say what you're thankful for. Expressing gratitude creates individual happiness and focuses children on the health and hope of a situation. This is an important part of the reappraisal strategy which supports mental health. Reappraisal is a way of replacing negative thinking with more hopeful and kind interpretation of a situation. Expressing gratitude helps focus thinking on positive parts of your child's day which nurtures healthier decision making.

Storytelling

Sometimes morning routines do not go well despite our best efforts. It's at these times that storytelling can be used to create a more positive routine. I developed a strategy called wild puppy/calm puppy while working as a social worker. You will need a couple of pictures to show your child: one picture of a puppy or animal acting in a wild way and one picture of a happy and calm animal. After school, you can show a picture of a puppy acting wildly and one that is calm. Show these pictures to your child and ask which puppy she saw in the morning. Your child may laugh and point to the puppy who looks a little wild. This brings your child in as the storyteller. You can then ask questions and explore the morning routine. Below are questions and statements that help children develop insight into their own behavior. This insight helps children develop better strategies for coping with morning transitions. This strategy also helps the conversation stay neutral and fun by externalizing the problem. This technique is very effective in helping children learn how to direct their behavior in a positive way. Children are creative and innovative with this type of conversation and puppy storytelling as it helps children find their own solution and develop positive ways to resolve a problem.

How can we keep your wild puppy heart focused during morning time routine?

What was wild puppy doing this morning that made routine difficult?

What would help wild puppy feel more calm and focused during morning routine?

How can we see more of the calm and happy puppy? Show picture of a calm puppy.

How does wild puppy feel during morning routine?

Morning Chart

needs work · good · great!

How did I do?   **1**   **2**   **3**

	Sunday	Monday	Tuesday	Wednesday	Thursday	Friday	Saturday

Deep belly breaths help me feel **happy and calm**.

	Sunday	Monday	Tuesday	Wednesday	Thursday	Friday	Saturday

shirt · pants · getting dressed

I am dressed and ready for **a wonderful day**.

	Sunday	Monday	Tuesday	Wednesday	Thursday	Friday	Saturday

breakfast

I am **thankful** for this day.

	Sunday	Monday	Tuesday	Wednesday	Thursday	Friday	Saturday

tooth brush · comb · soap

I can take **care of myself**.

	Sunday	Monday	Tuesday	Wednesday	Thursday	Friday	Saturday

backpack · lunch · shoes.

Anything is possible today.

Morning Chart Supportive Statements

Positive words support emotional regulation while negative words heighten symptoms of A.D.H.D. Here are some statements that help children feel proud about their effort to follow a schedule.

I liked the positive words you used this morning. Your words have the power to make wonderful things happen.

It was very grown up of you to pick your own clothes and get ready for school without too many reminders.

I noticed that you looked at the chart to remind yourself of the next step.

I liked the way you used the morning chart to keep yourself focused and organized.

I was proud of you for moving through morning routine even though you wanted to stay in bed.

I liked the way you smiled and started the morning with positive words.

You used your words to say how you felt this morning. This helped me understand why you were upset about getting up this morning.

What sparkle activity could we use to have a more peaceful morning?

Is there a sparkly activity that helps make morning routine a success?

Homework Routine

This homework routine creates an environment of focus and calm by using specific visuals and words helpful to children struggling with learning and school. It also ties in relaxation techniques that help children manage homework-related anxiety. Homework can be stressful and create tension between parent and child. Children may struggle with focus or become discouraged about their ability to understand and complete an assignment. This routine helps children adopt a growth mindset which supports and celebrates children's effort and creativity. Process-based praise is the perfect antidote to the increasing pressure on children to succeed and avoid failure.

Many of the words and statements being used with children reflect our own anxiety and worry about their progress. A research project by Jean Twenge, PhD, professor of psychology at San Diego State University noticed a sharp increase in anxiety and depression in our children. The pressure and difficult language we use with our children plays a role in this rise of emotional problems. This section on homework provides research and examples on the most supportive and powerful words to share with your child to incite belief in themselves as learners while helping them develop positive emotional skills.

Relaxation

It's helpful to take a deep breath and do some belly breathing or muscle relaxation before starting homework. Breathing in fully and deeply brings a sense of calm as more oxygen is getting delivered to the body and brain. There is a chart titled *Relax My Body* that helps children relax and focus on homework.

Science of Animal Pictures

Taking a moment together to look at cute animal pictures and having a snack helps create a fun and relaxed homework environment. Cute pictures of animals activates parts of the brain that deliver tranquility and calm. Hioshi Nittono, PhD, led a research study on focus and the brain. Dr. Nittono found that when children see a picture of a cute animal their memory improved and children's dexterity and speed at mental tasks also improved. Scientists in Japan found that children who looked at pictures of cute animals did better on games that require focus and attention. Looking at funny or cute animal pictures together builds connection and empathy between parent and child. It's easier to start a difficult homework assignment if you have had a chance to laugh and connect.

Homework

Your child can spend a few moments organizing his papers and workspace so he feels prepared when starting homework. It can be helpful to do some work yourself while your child is studying. For example, you can write out a grocery list while your child is studying. You can plan with your child about how long the assignment or homework will take. I use candy, or items from nature as a marker for each unit of time passed. I use a mason jar to put candy or the fun object in to represent a measure of time. Your child can see the passage of time with this strategy. Children enjoy putting a marble or starburst for each five, ten or fifteen minutes of time that has passed. Tracking time helps children with A.D.H.D. develop time management and organization skills.

Process-Based Praise

Types of praise and the way we comment on a child's effort and behavior influence whether a child will work hard or give up. Stanford researcher, Carol Dweck, PhD, has been studying motivation and perseverance since the 1960's. She found that children who were praised for their innate talent gave up more easily than children who were complimented for specific behavior. Process-based praise is a compliment focused on the behavior and effort of a person. Children who are given process-based praise are more resilient and continue to work hard and focus even when given a difficult task. A study led by Dr. Dweck found that children at 14 months old who heard process-based praise were more likely at age 7 or 8 to feel that they could learn and do anything if they put their mind to it while kids who were told they were naturally talented did not have the same focus and drive. Using specific process-based praise helps children create a positive override of a difficult situation and helps children believe that hard work and perserverance will lead to eventual success. Children at any age are inspired and motivated when they hear and begin to internalize process-based praise.

Organizing Papers and Desk

It can be challenging for children with A.D.H.D. to organize their desk and papers. Children, though, are open to questions and exploration about their desk. It can be very helpful to use a storytelling technique about your child's desk or workspace at home. Have him tell you why his space is organized, or not, as it is and discuss together how it might be a more effective homework space. This process allows children to improve their organization at home and becomes a skill that transfers to school. Children with attention difficulties begin to thrive and move forward with each step toward organization.

Homework Chart

needs work   good   great!

How did I do?   **1**   **2**   **3**

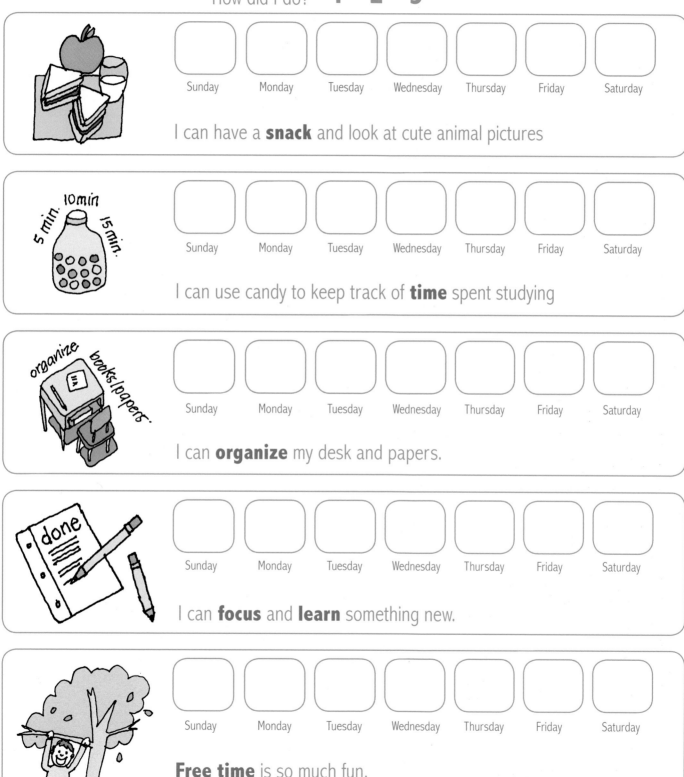

	Sunday	Monday	Tuesday	Wednesday	Thursday	Friday	Saturday

I can have a **snack** and look at cute animal pictures

	Sunday	Monday	Tuesday	Wednesday	Thursday	Friday	Saturday

I can use candy to keep track of **time** spent studying

	Sunday	Monday	Tuesday	Wednesday	Thursday	Friday	Saturday

I can **organize** my desk and papers.

	Sunday	Monday	Tuesday	Wednesday	Thursday	Friday	Saturday

I can **focus** and **learn** something new.

	Sunday	Monday	Tuesday	Wednesday	Thursday	Friday	Saturday

Free time is so much fun.

Homework Supportive Statements

Listed below are examples of process-based praise. This type of praise will help your child creatively solve problems when facing challenges or setbacks. These statements below help children see their role in developing skills and establishing a mindset that helps them learn and adapt to new experiences.

I appreciate that you try even when things are hard.

You can do amazing things when you put your mind to it.

The things you work hard on help you succeed.

You learn something new each day.

You are learning and getting better each time you practice.

I like the confidence you showed when starting your homework.

Your positive words and thoughts are helping you do great things.

I make mistakes too.

I am proud of you for keeping your desk organized. What skills did you use to organize your papers and books this week?

Mistakes help us learn and grow.

I see that you want to do a good job.

Keep working on little things and you will be blessed by positive rewards.

You have worked hard and developed so many talents.

I like all the thought you put into solving this problem.

I am proud that you remembered to bring your homework home.

You are remembering more and more things.

Your memory gets stronger every time you practice something new.

Your brain remembers mistakes and works to find new solutions.

Dinner Routine

Having dinner together and sharing family stories develops and nurtures children's emotional health. Children who eat together as a family are less likely to drink, smoke, do drugs, attempt suicide or develop eating disorders. Research also shows that children who eat together have larger vocabularies, have better manners and are healthier. The most comprehensive survey done on this topic was through the University of Michigan which found that the frequency of eating meals at home as a family was the single biggest predictor of that child's academic achievement and positive behavioral health.

Sitting together at dinner is another way to develop focus and social skills. Children who watch TV while eating are learning to be distracted which can create tension and anxiety in the evening. Kids are more likely to be calm, set the table and wait patiently if they are involved in the process and can take ownership of dinnertime routine. Having your child place a positive note for a family member or decorate the table can help nurture a smooth and fun dinnertime. The appreciation notes show understanding and gratitude toward others. Having your children focus on what they like about others helps them develop emotional skills and deepens family bonds.

Expressing Gratitude and Sharing

Prayer or expressing gratitude helps create a calm eating environment and helps with the transition to dinnertime. Children who have a spiritual life and connect with family spiritually are 40% more likely to be protected from depression and anxiety. It's important to spend at least one time a day sitting and connecting as a family. The ritual of sitting down and sharing stories reduces stress and helps children learn to focus. It's clear that dinnertime plays a huge role in our children's success in so many areas of life. The stories and types of conversation we share greatly influence our children's emotional health and resiliency. For example, sharing stories about relatives and family helps children feel part of a larger community and may help them flourish under difficult circumstances.

Family Stories

Sharing family stories heals friction, anger and discord between parents and children. Bruce Feiler, author of The Secrets of Happy Families, writes that growing up and learning about your family history is the #1 predictor of a child's emotional well-being. As a social worker, I found that the most fun and easy way to resolve tension and anger in the home was by helping families listen and tell family stories. The board game called *Life Stories* is a great tool to use at dinner to help facilitate conversation. *Life Stories* is a game that asks questions and nurtures conversations about family. The unique and soulful questions help families create a wider understanding of each family member. You can take 3 to 4 cards out of the game and use them to facilitate dinner time conversation.

Research

Psychologist Sarah Marshall, PhD, made an interesting observation while working with children with learning disabilities. Dr. Marshall found that children who knew the most about their families were the most resilient and best able to handle difficult situations. She and several other colleagues found that the more children knew about their family's history the stronger their sense of control over their lives was. This family knowledge was also found to positively influence self-esteem and self-confidence. Psychologists found that family stories reflecting an individual's ability to handle or even thrive after a set back were the most powerful family narrative. These stories help children create resiliency, self-confidence and family connection. It's helpful to have children tell stories at dinner about their favorite memories and share the good and not so good parts their day.

As a social worker, I see how anger and conflict lessen over time by sitting down and sharing family stories. I recommend the board game *Life Stories* and encourage you to share your stories about how family takes care of on another.

Dinner Chart

How did I do?   **1**   **2**   **3**

Sunday	Monday	Tuesday	Wednesday	Thursday	Friday	Saturday

Washing my hands keeps me **healthy**.

Sunday	Monday	Tuesday	Wednesday	Thursday	Friday	Saturday

I can make the table look **beautiful**.

Sunday	Monday	Tuesday	Wednesday	Thursday	Friday	Saturday

I show **respect** and **kindness** by using my manners.

Sunday	Monday	Tuesday	Wednesday	Thursday	Friday	Saturday

It is nice to share **family** stories.

Sunday	Monday	Tuesday	Wednesday	Thursday	Friday	Saturday

I can help **clean up** after dinner.

Dinner Questions and Supportive Statements

The following is a list of ideas for conversation that incorporate the notion of family story telling. These statements help conversation that supports and nurtures emotional well-being. It's helpful for parents to share their own childhood stories to children as a way of nurturing empathy and insight into helpful behavior.

Your kindness today reminds me of my mother's kindness. Let me explain

You have a sense of humor like your uncle. That reminds me of a story.

I like the way you helped set the table. It makes dinnertime a joy.

Tell your children about an adventure your parents had growing up.

Tell your children how you met their mother or father.

Talk to your children about one of your favorite childhood memories.

Tell about someone in your family that remained hopeful when faced with a difficult situation.

Questions to pose that support children's emotional and spiritual needs.

Who do you think is especially wise in our family?

What was the most helpful way you saw someone handle a difficult situation?

Tell about a time you saw deep kindness from a family member.

Why do you think God wants us to work together as a family?

How can families show kindness and love toward each other?

What were the best things and worst things that happened today?

Was there a time during the day that you felt God's protection?

Bedtime Routine

Each one of these routines can serve as an assessment tool on how your family is doing. For example, when a child is not going to bed well it may mean he or she is feeling anxious and is unable to relax. Bedtime is another opportunity to share stories and develop important emotional skills. I recommend putting elementary school aged children to bed at 8:00pm and start the bedtime routine at 7pm. Children's A.D.H.D. symptoms can improve as much as 20% by getting enough rest at night. Getting adequate sleep allows children to enter dream state which helps regulate and develop organizational skills. Sleep helps with memory, and calms the parasympathetic-sympathetic nervous center. This helps children wake up the next day calm and focused.

Snack Time

It's nice to have a light snack so the stomach doesn't have to work so hard during the night. It's helpful to put a kind note or strength card next to their snack to create a positive transition to nighttime routine. It's important to unplug from electronics and TV at least one hour before bedtime to allow for a peaceful and relaxed transitions to bed. Research shows that children sleep 30 minutes more a night when there are no electronics in their bedroom.

Preparing for Bedtime Routine

It's important to look at the bedtime chart together and ask your child what needs to be done next. Your child may like to check each step off with a pen when he or she is done. It is deeply comforting for children to look at visual lists. If the bedtime routine becomes stressful, looking at cute animals hugging may help children feel calmer and happier. A research study from the University of Exeter in England found that looking at photos of people or animals hugging created a sense of calm and kindness. It can be helpful to choose a couple of sweet hugging animal pictures for bedtime to help with the transition to bed.

Bath Time

Taking a warm bath 30 minutes before bed helps the transition to sleep. It's helpful to take a warm bath and then go to bed in a somewhat chilly bedroom. This is another time to use aromatherapy to calm the body and mind. This heat exchange helps stimulate the pineal gland which produces melatonin. The optimum temperature for sleep is somewhere between 65 to 67 degrees. Meditation and smelling something pleasant are two ways to help reduce worry and stress in the evening time. Using Epson Salt in the bath calms the nervous system and has been found to be especially helpful for children with A.D.H.D.

PJ's and Brushing Teeth

It's nice to have pajamas laid out and tooth brush and tooth paste within easy reach. Having PJ's laid out on the bed helps children make the visual connection for the next step and allows for success in completing the final step of bedtime routine.

Family Stories

Storytelling is a soothing nighttime ritual that develops empathy and bonding between parent and child. It's the one time during the day that is quiet, slow and free from tasks and things that need to be done. This is a nice time to share your childhood memories and bring them to life through stories. These stories nurture a deeper understanding and bond that helps family's better cope with daily struggles. Telling joyful stories about fun family memories while doing belly breathing helps calm the mind.

I found as a social worker and as a mom that positive and fun stories help develop empathy and kindness between parent and child. Children are soulful and open to deeper conversations at night. Stories help children focus on happy memories as a way of calming the body and mind.

Bedtime Routine Chart

needs work   good   great!

How did I do?   **1**   **2**   **3**

Sunday	Monday	Tuesday	Wednesday	Thursday	Friday	Saturday

Snack time starts my bedtime **routine**.

Sunday	Monday	Tuesday	Wednesday	Thursday	Friday	Saturday

It is nice to **relax** and feel **calm**.

Sunday	Monday	Tuesday	Wednesday	Thursday	Friday	Saturday

I am almost ready for **bed**.

Sunday	Monday	Tuesday	Wednesday	Thursday	Friday	Saturday

Smelling something nice helps me **relax**.

Sunday	Monday	Tuesday	Wednesday	Thursday	Friday	Saturday

You are a **gift** from **God.**

Supportive Words and Statements for Bedtime Routine

Here are some supportive words and statements for nighttime. Children are especially open to positive affirmations and supportive stories at nighttime. It's helpful to talk about how much you enjoy and love your child.

I am proud of the positive words you used today.

I enjoyed spending time with you today.

Relax your mind and body and soon you will feel ready for sleep.

I am proud of you for taking care of yourself and getting ready for bed.

I feel happy when I am with you.

The happiest day was when God gave me you.

You can calm your body and mind.

You can choose a sparkle activity to help you relax.

You can put your hand on your belly and feel your belly rise and fall with each slow breath.

You are strong and healthy.

Tell your child about a fun family memory or a fun adventure growing up.

House Meeting

The house meeting chart uses pictures and words to help families connect and review progress with daily routines. It's helpful to have the house meeting on Sunday so that you can prepare for the upcoming week. A house meeting is a helpful time to show gratitude, look at individual strengths and review how your family did during times of transition and routine. House meetings tie in all the necessary elements that support family life while also connecting and bonding with one another. The measures for each routine help families reflect on the past week. For example, families can look at how many great efforts have been received for homework and explore the behaviors used to make this routine a success. If there was a struggle with a routine being reflected with the assessment 'needs work,' you can look at what behaviors or thinking could improve this routine.

Gratitude

This is a helpful time to express gratitude for the week and for family support. This can reinforce the behavior you liked and explore strategies to help each other stay on track during the following week.

Strengths

The pictures of strengths help keep routines running smoothly by identifying what tools are making your family strong or ones that family members may want to develop. These are strengths of character that help develop kindness, empathy and team work. The strengths following this section help children make choices that are in line with values that support kindness. It's helpful for each family member to choose a strength that he or she want to focus on during the week.

Manage Stress

In a survey of a thousand families, Ellen Galinsky, President and Co-Founder of the Families and Work Institute, found that children want parents to be less stressed, even more than spending more time with them. The house meeting is an amazing place to address stress and explore strategies for taking care of each other. It's helpful to choose a sparkle activity on the sparkle chart to support positive self-care.

Science and Research

Scientists at the University of California and elsewhere found that children who plan their own time, set weekly goals and evaluate their work build up the pre-frontal cortex and other parts of the brain that help them exert greater cognitive control over their lives. House meetings help children organize themselves and take greater pride in the week running smoothly. Children who are a part of the planning and communication about routines and addressing stress are more willing to work hard to make positive changes in their family.

Chores

The last step is choosing a chore. Chores are a helpful and important part of working together and creates closeness among family members. Having meaningful work where family members help each other supports children in becoming healthy adults. Sweden does especially well bringing children to adulthood as they all have unique jobs and responsibilities to help support their family. In the book, Parenting Beyond Borders, the author cites research on how children who do chores have a more peaceful and easy relationship with parents as they enter their teens.

House Meeting Questions

Here are some questions that help families reflect on some of the daily routines. These questions help develop insight and problem solving skills that support families working as a team.

What role did you play in making one of the routines go smoothly?

How did the routines go this week?

Was there a sparkly activity that helped with morning or bedtime routine?

Did you learn something new about a family member this week?

Was there a person who was especially helpful during one of the routines?

What chore would you like this week?

House Meeting

Talk with family about things for which you are **thankful**.

Choose a **strength** card that you want to **focus** on this week.

How were the **routines** this week?

How did **you** do?

How can **we** work better **together**?

What do we need to do to make a **routine** run more smoothly?

What should we do in the coming week to **celebrate** progress?

Strengths

joyful

loving

write what you love

relax

take responsibility

brave

curious

thankful

create fun

hopeful

try something new

strong effort
with routine

learn from
mistakes

helpful

express feelings

peaceful

energized

smile

Chores Chart

How can you be **helpful?** **1** **2** **3**

Sunday	Monday	Tuesday	Wednesday	Thursday	Friday	Saturday

I will **walk** the dog.

Sunday	Monday	Tuesday	Wednesday	Thursday	Friday	Saturday

I can **clean** the bathroom.

Sunday	Monday	Tuesday	Wednesday	Thursday	Friday	Saturday

I can **organize** my room.

Sunday	Monday	Tuesday	Wednesday	Thursday	Friday	Saturday

I **vacuum** and make the room sparkle.

Sunday	Monday	Tuesday	Wednesday	Thursday	Friday	Saturday

It is **helpful** when I take out the garbage.

Chores Chart

needs work   good   great!

How can you be **helpful?**   1   2   3

	Sunday	Monday	Tuesday	Wednesday	Thursday	Friday	Saturday

I can **wash** the dishes.

I can **pack** a lunch.

I can **organize** my desk and papers.

I can **put away** laundry.

I can **make** my bed.

Emotional Skills

The chart titled *Feelings Change Like The Weather* is a wheel with seven feelings represented by different weather conditions. I use the many types of weather to represent and bring light to the changing nature of moods and emotions. The feeling of gratitude is represented with stars in the night sky, worried with lightening, happiness with a rainbow, hope with a sun emerging from the clouds, strong with a full sun anger with a tornado and sad is represented with rain. Research shows that merely assigning a name or label to how we feel calms down the circuitry in the right hemisphere of the brain. The seven weather types help children understand and tell stories related to how they feel. Here is a brief description of each of the seven emotions and storytelling strategies that help children direct their behavior in a positive way.

Anger and Sadness: It's helpful to talk about the elements that come together to create rain or clouds and compare these to the elements that influence how we feel. For example, the elements that make up anger may be a feeling in the body, or thinking of past hurts or frustrations. This awareness helps children better understand and influence how they feel.

Gratitude and Hope: The story of pathfinders is a beautiful way to help children feel hope and express gratitude to all the helpers in their lives. Pathfinders are people living in remote areas who provide directions, food or kind words to weary travelers. Pathfinders expect nothing in return and are happy to support hikers in finding their way. It's helpful to talk about other pathfinders such as a teacher or a kind friend whose care has helped them find their best path.

Happiness: Children with A.D.H.D. may have difficulty creating a peaceful environment. Helping children be in the moment and using sensory experiences such as music, art activities and aromatherapy are some solutions that help children feel more content and happy. Mendability is an amazing online program that offers art and play activities that nurtures the emotional health of children with A.D.H.D. and other learning differences.

Worry and Strong: Children with A.D.H.D. may be hearing negative words. These negative words fuel worry and anxiety. Expressing love and using strength-based praise with your child reduces stress and anxiety in children and adults. Emotional coaching helps children to process feelings and supports intellectual and emotional growth. Asking children questions about how they feel is the best way to coach and support children in finding strong and helpful solutions.

Feelings Change like the Weather

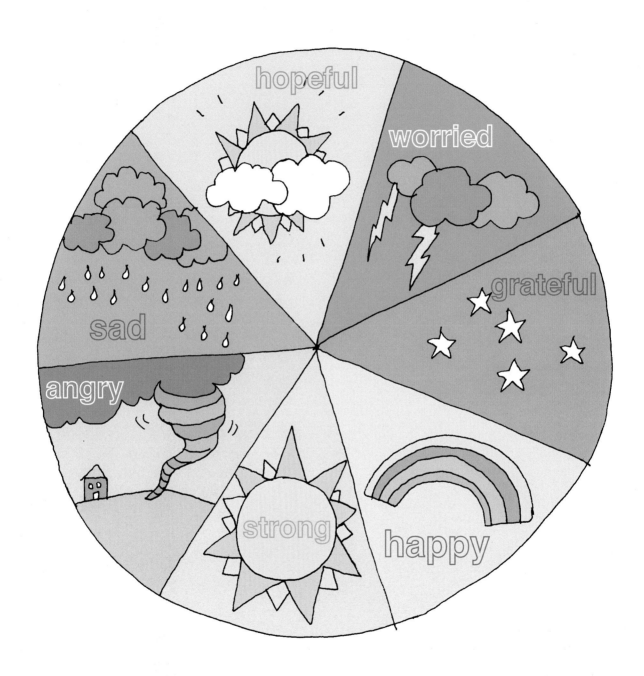

How do you feel today?

Statements That Help Children Understand Their Feelings

Here are some helpful statements and supportive words to help children better understand their feelings. Talking about feelings or emotional coaching help children weather different emotions and promote emotional intelligence.

What makes you feel sad?

What makes you feel Happy?

What makes you feel angry?

What makes you feel happy?

What makes you feel anxious?

What makes you feel this way?

Let's learn more about this feeling.

Let's get curious about this feeling. This will help us find solutions.

You can notice signs of getting angry sooner next time.

You can ask for help when you don't know what to do.

You had a hard time handling anger the way you wanted.

Is there someone that you know that handles strong emotions well? What are some of the strategies that they use?

What is pushing you into the tornado of anger and what do you need to get out?

Describe a situation or words that make you feel happy or hopeful.

What can you do to create happiness for yourself?

What steps can you take to feel calmer?

That's your angry voice, what does your hopeful voice tell you.

Let's make a list of some people who care about you.

How can I be helpful to you?

Sparkle Activity

A *sparkle activity* is a fun way to help children find solutions and strategies to cope with strong emotions or frustration that may surface during difficult transitions of the day. These two sparkle charts allow children to choose and make daily habits of self-care. I have a set of strategies represented in a wheel and in a chart, both entitled sparkle activities. The sparkle activities can help children respond positively to difficult situations. The sparkle chart is helpful to look at while moving through daily routines such as morning or homework. You can ask your child to choose a sparkle activity that will make morning, homework, dinner or evening routine feel calmer and run more smoothly. In the book <u>Your Fantastic Elastic Brain</u>, author JoAnn Deak, PhD, talks about how the brain grows and develops more dendrites, or signal receivers, when a child continues to push forward when something is difficult. Children who believe that they can influence their feelings are better equipped to handle setbacks in childhood and into adulthood. Listed below are some ways for children to self-sooth.

Exercise: Moving the body helps burn up extra cortisol, which helps decrease anxious feelings. Exercise is a proven method of managing stress and has a protective mechanism that follows even into times of rest. It helps to talk to your child about which exercise they like best and ways to incorporate this into your daily schedule. Exercise increases dopamine, which helps with focus and concentration.

Smell: Olfactory nerves link directly to the brain's limbic system. The olfactory nerve is your sense of smell that can influence your emotional health. The limbic system is what governs your emotions and memory. Some science finds that the smell of orange can calm and reduce anxious feelings.

Music: Music fires up synapses in the brain which increase the neurochemical dopamine. This results in better attention, memory and motivation. Having your child sit and listen to classical music on headphones is a powerful exercise. Listening to classical music may help manage emotions, and develops many executive function skills such as focus and motivation.

Play: Play helps children relax and develop important emotional regulation skills. Certain sensory play such playing with warm play dough helps children feel calm and learn to focus on an activity. Putting a puzzle together helps children with A.D.H.D. develop focus and organization skills. Putting a larger puzzle together can be a fun family activity.

Kindness: In a study children ages 9-11 years old were asked to do three kind things a week such as a write a letter to friend, help out with chores or use positive words toward someone. Children who did three kind things a week, especially if the three acts of kindness happened all in one day, reported an increase in happiness and greater popularity at school. Being positive and kind creates hope and activates the reward circuitry. Children are better willing to listen and focus when hearing a 3 -1 balance of positive versus negative words. Using kindness and empathy helps children work on goals and feel motivated to keep trying.

Sparkle Activities

relaxing bath

smell something nice

eat healthy
protein
fruit
vegetables
grains
dairy

MILK

thank you

show gratitude

move your body

listen to soothing music

journal what you love

Pick an activity to brighten your mood?

Sparkle chart

Which activity helps you **sparkle**?   **1**   **2**   **3**

Sunday	Monday	Tuesday	Wednesday	Thursday	Friday	Saturday

Send a letter with **kind words** daily or weekly.

Sunday	Monday	Tuesday	Wednesday	Thursday	Friday	Saturday

Move your body and **feel better**.

Sunday	Monday	Tuesday	Wednesday	Thursday	Friday	Saturday

Listen to classical music to **soothe the mind**.

Sunday	Monday	Tuesday	Wednesday	Thursday	Friday	Saturday

Believe in your ability to **improve and grow**.

Sunday	Monday	Tuesday	Wednesday	Thursday	Friday	Saturday

Breathe in and out slowly and feel your belly rise and fall.

Helping Children Find Solutions for Anxiety

Here are some statements to help sooth children when they are feeling anxious. These statements are powerful in diffusing some of the triggers for anxiety, which can make daily transitions and routines difficult. The following words nurture and support children during emotional ups and downs and creates a sense of safety when they feel lonely or hopeless.

We can work together to find a solution.

I'll stay close until you feel better.

I love you, you are safe.

Let's smell a nice scent and wrap up in a warm blanket.

Close your eyes and I will tell you a nice story.

Let's think of all the people who love and care for you.

I want to help you.

Let's pretend your worry is passing you by on a cloud.

Let's make up a story about how your problem could be solved.

Choose a sparkle activity that will help you feel better.

Let me sing to you and hold you.

What words help you feel strong?

What thoughts help you feel hopeful?

Feeling Signals

The feeling signal chart helps children manage stress. Conflicts and strong emotions can serve as learning opportunities for children to develop important emotional and social skills. Children are best equipped to handle difficult situations and stress when they talk about how they feel. Paul Eckman, PhD, a leading researcher of emotions, talks about anger being a sign of some interference in daily life. The following chart helps children stop on cue and identify self-soothing strategies that can remove a feeling or situation that is interfering in their lives. Helping children stop on cue and respond positively to strong emotions help develops their cognitive control. Children with A.D.H.D. have difficulty with executive function skills, also known as cognitive control. The 'stop, caution and go' steps help children develop important executive function skills like focus, impulse control and problem solving.

Stop: Children can look at the stop signal and identify stressors or a strong emotion they are experiencing. Exploring feelings helps calm the nervous system, leading the way to better insight and social awareness. Stopping on cue strengthens and rewires the brain. In the book Focus, Daniel Goleman talks about how stopping on cue literally rewires the brain for greater ability to focus and organize thoughts.

Caution: Executive function skills are housed in the prefrontal cortex of the brain which functions better at times of calm. There are no lights on in the pre-frontal cortex at times of stress. Deep breathing is the best strategy for calming the mind and body. Your child can use deep breathing to calm the effects of stress.

GO: This is a helpful time to use hopeful words and coach your child to breathe deeply. You can put a stuffed animal on your belly to show how the belly rises and falls with each breath. You can talk about a path angel who helped you and support your child in visualizing a time someone was loving or caring to them.

Feeling Signals

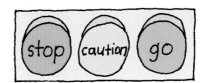

strong anger may be a signal that you need help to calm your body

 stop and tell someone how you feel

 sad   worried   angry

 negative self talk may be causing you to feel angry

 use healing words

breathe in for 4 seconds   breathe out for 4 seconds
repeat until you feel better

 breathe while thinking of all things for which you are grateful

Relax my Body

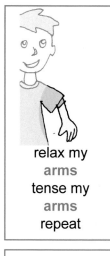

relax my
arms
tense my
arms
repeat

relax my
forehead
tense my
forehead
repeat

relax my
face
tense my
face
repeat

relax my
shoulders
tense my
shoulders
repeat

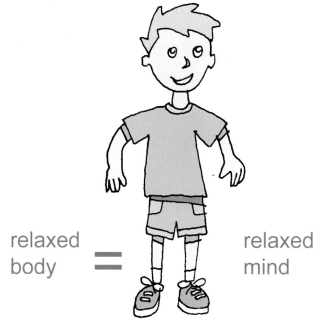

relaxed body = relaxed mind

relax my
hands
tense my
hands
repeat

relax my
tummy
tense my
tummy
repeat

relax my
feet
tense my
feet
repeat

relax my
legs
tense my
legs
repeat

Supportive Statements and Questions to Help Children Feel Better

Here are some supportive statements to use with your child when they are feeling overwhelmed or alone.

Who was your path angel this week?

Close your eyes and I will tell you a nice story

Breathe deeply and feel your belly rise and fall.

You are strong and healthy.

You can calm your mind and body.

I am happy when I am with you.

Tell me about a time when you felt God's protection.

The happiest day was when God gave me you.

You can notice when your body feels tense, then relax your shoulders and breathe.

That was a stressful situation and it was hard to know what to do.

What role do you play in creating your own happiness?

Questions that help children better understand their feelings

When do you notice this feeling the most?

Where are you when you feel this way? School or home?

What steps can you take to feel better?

What thoughts help you feel hopeful?

What words or thoughts help you feel strong?

That's your angry voice. What does your hopeful voice say?

Statements that help children develop insight and empathy

Anger can help us see that this is a moment that our body and mind need quiet.

You are strong enough to sit with this difficult feeling.

I liked the way you pushed angry thoughts away and brought hope in?

It's okay to have anger. It's just your mind at work.

You did a good job asking questions and learning more about what to do next time.

Let's get curious about why you got so angry. This will help us find solutions.

You can ask for help if you don't know what to do.

You had a hard time handling anger the way you wanted. You can do better next time.

I am worried about you and want to help.

I am proud of you.

This feeling will pass.

Let's pretend that we are blowing out a candle.

We will work together to find a solution.

I'll stay close to you until you feel better.

Conclusion

As a social worker, I found pictures to have a unique and beautiful way of teaching and nurturing children to use their creativity. Anxiety and stress is high in children with A.D.H.D. due to the pressure to succeed and difficulty in regulating their own sensory environment. As a parent, I wanted to motivate and inspire my own son to use his creativity to grow and learn. It's clear that anxiety interferes with motivation and can make children feel hopeless in the face of new learning. Paying attention to one positive picture or listening to a story helps children focus on the present moment. Focusing on the present moves children away from anxious thoughts and insulates them from stress. Words that focus on effort helps restore children's hope in themselves as learners.

Statements and questions using process-based praise is uniquely helpful to children with attention difficulties and learning differences. Process-based praise allows children with A.D.H.D. to use the creativity and energy to learn from mistakes. These picture charts teach daily living strategies and reinforce learning for children.

Positive words, structured daily routines and pictures come together to help children understand the deeper meaning of stories and events. I started using pictures, process-based praise and storytelling to help my clients better understand and follow the structure of daily routines. The pictures and words in these daily charts help children better understand the structure of the day and develop insight into their own behavior. These picture charts also help children bypass some of the difficulties they may have with reading and understanding social situations. Using the emotional skills charts and daily routine charts on a regular basis help children thrive and develop important cognitive skills.

Listening to stories and positive words activate the senses, emotions and memories across the entire brain. The picture charts in this book help children develop spatial and social reasoning and develop executive function skills. Children with A.D.H.D. need structure to learn basic developmental, emotional and social skills. Children begin to understand routines once they relate them to pictures and are mixed with creativity and fun. Relating to nature, aromatherapy, art, positive words, and storytelling helps children with A.D.H.D. use their creatively and enthusiasm to stay motivated and on task.

Children do not respond well to the high pressure and negative environment that is pressing in on most of us. Engaging the senses and connecting as a family protects children from the pressures of a busy and stressful school experience. Simple strategies such as breathing deeply while focusing on relaxing thoughts help children develop planning and emotional skills. The morning, homework, dinner and nighttime routines help children manage stress and learn new ways to organize their thoughts and behavior. Positive words and structure help children become more resilient as they learn new tools and strategies to move through the transitions of the day. Telling stories helps bring these visuals and charts to life. Children are more willing to collaborate and share their feelings with an adult who asks their child to share or tell a story.

Focusing on children's effort, and finding time to connect is powerful in the lives of all children. Unplugging from technology, developing emotional skills and learning organizational tools helps children with A.D.H.D. become resilient in the face of difficulty. Families need support, kindness and structure to ease into the next transition of the day. Pictures, organization and praise shine light on all the effort that goes into developing new and important emotional and developmental skills.

We can use kind words, inspiring stories and fun pictures to help children become strong and hopeful in the challenges associated with A.D.H.D. Children will internalize this kindness and use hopeful language to transcend difficulties and hardships. Organization and nurturing the emotional lives of children helps families feel happy and supported.

Resources

Here are books and resources that are uniquely helpful to families of children with A.D.H.D. The following resources helped me reinforce the organization and structure that my clients were seeking to minimize the symptoms of A.D.H.D.

Mendability Therapy is a research-based program that helps children learn to focus based on the principals of neuroplasticity. It's a simple online program that uses fun sensory games and activities to teach important developmental skills.

Craneo Sacral Massage Therapy is a type of massage that helps regulate and calm the nervous system.

Bibliography

Biel Lindsey, and Peske Nancy, Raising a Sensory Smart Child, Penguin Books, 2009

Block, Douglas, The Power of Positive Talk, Words to Help Every Child Succeed, Free Spirit Publishing, 2003

Cowen Scott Stephen, Fire Child Water Child, New Harbinger Publication, INC, copy right 2012

Dweck S. Carol, Mindset, The New Psychology of Success, Ballantine Books, NY, 2006

Feiler, Bruce, The Secrets of Happy Families, Harper Collins publisher, copyright 2013

Golman, Daniel, Focus, The Hidden Driver of Excellence, Harper Collins Publishers, 2013

In John Gottman's Book Raising Emotionally Intelligent Children, he has a list of important books to read to children to nurture and support emotional and social intelligence. This list of children's books help children develop insight and improve impulsivity through awareness. Author Lori Lite also writes beautiful children's books that teach mindfulness and relaxation strategies.

About the Author

Katie Unterreiner graduated from Portland State University with a Masters in Social Work and is a Licensed Clinical Social Worker (LCSW). After graduation, Katie worked at Options Counseling for ten years providing in-home counseling to children and families. Through her work with these clients, and informed by the critical research of other leaders in the field, Katie developed a series of charts and visual tools to use as she created and led social emotional skills groups for children with special needs. This toolkit became the foundation for her first book, Motivate, which is written with the goal of helping all children gain the emotional and behavioral skills to thrive.

About the Illustrator

Jerome Unterreiner (Katie's husband) is an architect and urban designer by training and a wonderful illustrator by coincidence. Jerome practices globally with an urban planning and place-making focus on health and wellness.

ISBN: 978-1-4834-6438-1 (sc)
ISBN: 978-1-4834-6439-8 (e)

Because of the dynamic nature of the Internet, any web addresses or links contained in this book may have changed since publication and may no longer be valid. The views expressed in this work are solely those of the author and do not necessarily reflect the views of the publisher, and the publisher hereby disclaims any responsibility for them.

Certain stock imagery © Thinkstock.

Illustrations by Jerome Unterreiner.

Lulu Publishing Services rev. date: 3/6/2017